# HR Outsourcing:
# the key decisions

Professor William Scott-Jackson
Tim Newham
Melanie Gurney

The Chartered Institute of Personnel and Development is the leading publisher of books and reports for personnel and training professionals, students, and all those concerned with the effective management and development of people at work. For full details of all our titles, please contact the Publishing Department:

Tel: 020 8612 6204

E-mail: publish@cipd.co.uk

To view and purchase all CIPD titles:
www.cipd.co.uk/bookstore

For details of CIPD research projects:
www.cipd.co.uk/research

# HR Outsourcing:
# the key decisions

Professor William Scott-Jackson

Tim Newham

Melanie Gurney

**Centre for Applied HR Research, Oxford Brookes University**

First published 2005

Cover design by Curve
Designed by Beacon GDT
Typeset by Paperweight
Printed in Great Britain by Short Run Press

*British Library Cataloguing in Publication Data*
A catalogue record for this book is available from the British Library

ISBN 1 84398 136 X

Chartered Institute of Personnel and Development,
151 The Broadway, London SW19 1JQ

Tel: 020 8612 6200
Website: www.cipd.co.uk

Incorporated by Royal Charter. Registered charity no. 1079797.

# Contents

# Acknowledgements

The CIPD would like to thank Professor William Scott-Jackson, Tim Newham and Melanie Gurney of the Centre for Applied HR Research, Oxford Brookes University for managing and preparing this Executive Briefing. We would also like to thank Professor Jean Woodall of Oxford Brookes University, academic adviser to the project.

The following organisations kindly contributed to the research as case study participants:

- Atos Origin

- Aviva

- BAE Systems

- BG Group plc

- BP

- BT

- Cable & Wireless

- CMi plc

- Dell

- Essex County Council

- Marconi

- Marks and Spencer

- NU Healthcare

- SPV Management Ltd

- Standard Chartered Bank

- T-Mobile

- UBS

The members of the project's working party (detailed below) are also thanked for their contributions:

| | |
|---|---|
| Malcolm Howard | Accenture |
| Chris Dickson | BAE |
| Louise Wallwork | BAE |
| Jenny Arwas | BT |

Joe McDavid          BT

Laurence Collins     Ceridian Centrefile

Stephanie Bird       Dell

Kit Cox              E-nate

Lorraine Cox         Essex County Council

Alan Little          Hay Group

Steve Foster         Northgate

Nigel Crainey        Ordnance Survey

Alan McKinnon        T-Mobile

Geoff Rogers         The Value Partnership

Hugh Morris          Xchanging

# List of figures and tables

# Foreword

This Executive Briefing has been produced by the Chartered Institute of Personnel and Development, in partnership with the Centre for Applied HR Research at Oxford Brookes University, to help UK organisations address some key questions about outsourcing HR activities. It is based on a search of existing practitioner and academic literature, as well as new research with a number of organisations that have practical and valuable stories to tell in relation to HR outsourcing.

HR functions are changing rapidly and have a desire to play a more strategic role in supporting organisational performance through more effective people management. But this requires improvements in HR administrative efficiency, be that through investment and exploitation of improved HR information systems (HRIS) or drawing on the technology and expertise of an external supplier. HR functions' current experience with HRIS is mixed: often it is reactive, and based on experience of working with unconnected systems.

Outsourcing aspects of HR is not new, for example, payroll. In recent years, there has been a lot of noise about its benefits and there have been several high-profile deals. However, the incidence of HR outsourcing still remains relatively low and some problems have also been reported. At the same time very little organisation-based research is available on the pros and cons of outsourcing. Therefore, the CIPD commissioned this work to address questions members are raising, such as: 'Should I be outsourcing?' and 'How do I decide what and how to outsource?'.

This Briefing addresses:

- How outsourcing is defined.

- Potential benefits of outsourcing.

- Potential pitfalls and alternatives to outsourcing.

- Decision-making regarding HR outsourcing.

- Selecting outsourcing providers.

- Managing the transition from in-house to outsourcing.

- Minimising risks and making outsourcing work.

The focus in this Briefing is on key decision-making and overall approach, rather than the detailed tools and techniques for implementation, which is where most of the existing literature concentrates. There is a References and Further Reading section at the back of the Briefing.

We hope that you find this Briefing useful and would be interested in hearing your reactions. So if you have any thoughts, please do let us know.

**Rebecca Clake and Vanessa Robinson**
Advisers, Organisation and Resourcing
Chartered Institute of Personnel and Development
(research@cipd.co.uk)

# Executive summary

The changing shape of the delivery of HR services in organisations has significant ramifications for the future of the HR function. HR outsourcing has received high levels of media attention in recent years, but the subject is highly controversial. The CIPD, therefore, felt that it would be timely to undertake research and provide written guidance in this area. This resulting Executive Briefing is aimed at ensuring that those HR and non-HR professionals, who have responsibility for developing and improving the delivery of HR services within their organisation, are aware of the full implications of going down the outsourcing route as well as possible alternative solutions. In particular, it addresses the strategic issues and decisions that need to be made when considering whether or not HR outsourcing is an appropriate response for the function.

The research has been case study-driven, and has identified, not surprisingly, that any decision and resulting solution is likely to be very situation-specific. Organisations' decisions may be informed by a combination of different factors.

Strategic drivers might include:

◘ reducing cost

◘ reducing risk

◘ increasing the effectiveness of HR delivery

◘ moving HR up the value-chain

◘ gaining commercial return

◘ flexibility of the HR service and associated costs

◘ lack of in-house expertise.

While other influencing factors include:

◘ cultural factors

◘ reaction to changing size/structure of the organisation

◘ prior experience of outsourcing other business functions.

Our case studies include organisations that have outsourced some or all of their HR processes and activities (and the resulting challenges that these decisions have brought, including whether or not to renew the contract), and also those organisations that have considered outsourcing, but decided not to pursue this route.

It is important to review thoroughly the costs and
benefits (both financial and non-financial)
associated with moving to outsourced HR. Time
needs to be spent, not only on selecting the most
appropriate supplier but on investing resources in
managing the transition to the new delivery
model. Ensuring HR and line managers have the
right skill sets and competencies to operate
effectively in this new environment is also critical.

Outsourcing is one manifestation of the
transforming shape of HR and, in particular, the
increasing demands being placed upon HR
functions to deliver greater levels of transactional
efficiency at the same time as raising the level of
other HR activity to focus on 'strategic', 'value-
adding' service. The CIPD believes that HR
functions need continually to improve the
efficiency of the administrative services they deliver,
as part of their shift to a more strategic and
influential future. Outsourcing is one potential
route to achieving this.

What is outsourcing? ▶ Potential drivers ▶ Potential pitfalls and alternatives ▶ Decision-making regarding HR outsourcing ▶ Selecting outsource providers ▶ Managing transition ▶ Minimising the risk and making outsourcing work

◘ **Definitions of outsourcing and HR outsourcing**

◘ **A short review of current literature on HR outsourcing and sources for further reading**

◘ **The difference between outsourcing, and other methods of getting HR work done outside the organisation**

# 1 | What is outsourcing?

Outsourcing is

*the delegation of one or more business processes to an external provider, who then owns, manages and administers the selected processes based on defined and measurable performance metrics (Gartner, 1995).*

Outsourcing has been on the agenda for HR departments for at least 10 years and is not a new phenomenon. Manufacturing operations have outsourced elements of their work since the middle of the twentieth century, and many companies have outsourced employee services like security, cleaning and catering for decades. In the 1990s, businesses strategies focused on shareholder value, and there was a move to business process re-engineering to realise service and cost efficiencies.

**Case study**

**Outsourcing and the need to integrate HR processes – BAE***

BAE Systems faced the need to integrate two HR infrastructures after a merger. Chris Dickson (project manager) said: 'A key driver was to reduce costs, and eliminate duplication of departments and roles, whilst maintaining levels of service.' In other words, BAE Systems was focusing its outsourcing plans on obtaining a more cost effective service, rather than a need to increase service quality.

First, Chris reviewed HR shared services, administration and basic support to line managers. BAE Systems considered retaining HR services in-house with support of external consultants, but finally concluded that it could only achieve step change by looking to a more holistic Business Process Outsourcing (BPO) solution, largely as a result of cultural challenges created by the merger. Accountabilities for the decision and implementation were shared between Chris, the senior management team, the Group HR Director (as internal 'champion' for the project) and the MDs, and HR Directors of the individual businesses.

BAE Systems created a joint venture with Xchanging in March/April 2000 to outsource non-customer-facing roles (ie including all HR administration functions, while excluding business partners, employee relations, strategy and policy).

BAE transferred 70 per cent of its HR staff to the Xchanging joint venture. 'We achieved our initial criteria of reducing costs and maintaining service and we now have less HR staff, who are now working at more strategic levels across the business', said Chris.

* Information supplied by Chris Dickson

**Case study**

**Outsourcing and coping with the growing workforce – CMi plc***

CMi plc decided to outsource HR because the company was growing very quickly, from 69 to 160 staff in about a year. As the company grew, it had the following choices:

1   to grow HR internally as the internal demand for HR services increased;

2   to up-skill the existing HR representative and outsource the HR administration tasks, or

3   to outsource the entire function.

At the time of decision, HR became the responsibility of the Finance Director, Lynne Hunt. 'My remit was to standardise the service level and improve quality of delivery', said Lynne. 'With the right strategy and management, our HR function could be a business benefit by helping us to attract, retain and develop our staff. We decided to outsource HR because we felt that we did not have the capabilities in-house to deliver the required level of service.'

CMi decided to outsource its entire HR provision, including strategy and communication, to Northgate Ltd. It now has a dedicated team of three HR staff (a senior consultant, consultant and administrator). The direct cost of HR provision increased because of the outsource, but Lynne considers the overall result to be cost-effective because the costs of developing HR in-house were avoided. As a pragmatic reason, CMi also saved office space – which was at a premium in this fast-growing company – by having HR delivered off-site.

Now, CMi has a much more professional service with clearly-defined strategy and policy. Lynne mentions that 'the HR service that we receive is continuing to improve as we learn how to get the best from our outsourcing relationship, and I consider the decision to be a cost-effective one'.

* Information supplied by Lynne Hunt

Outsourcing of HR activities has been a growth area over the past decade, as organisations have sought benefits in passing over labour-intensive, specialist, or non-core activities to a third party expert. The drivers of HR outsourcing are varied, including, for example, a desire to reduce costs, increase effectiveness, obtain external expertise or release internal HR expertise to focus on strategic issues and business partnering.

Organisations may outsource virtually all HR processes or, more commonly, select specific components such as payroll or resourcing. So far, very few organisations have outsourced their entire HR function. In large organisations it is most common to have outsourced the operational elements of delivering all HR activities but retain control over HR strategy and decision-making. Interestingly, small organisations often do the reverse, effectively outsourcing their strategy (to HR consultants and other professional advisers) and keeping the delivery of HR processes internal.

Outsourcing, therefore, is not only a strategy relevant to large organisations. Several providers now offer outsourced HR services to smaller organisations.

## HR outsourcing – the existing literature

The development of HR outsourcing has been greeted fairly positively (especially in the USA) by many HR and IT professional publications, but the justification made for HR outsourcing and the evaluation of its consequences is often weak or contradictory. For a start, there is a lack of clarity about what outsourcing really involves. The definitions used can be fairly elastic, stretching from the 'minimalist' sub-contracting of HR service delivery to an external provider, to 'spin-off' joint ventures or 'shared services, and more recently 'business process outsourcing' (Lawler *et al*, 2004). When authors adopt very different definitions, this can in turn pose problems in establishing the effects of HR outsourcing (Kakabadse and Kakabadse, 2002; Klaas *et al*, 2001).

To date, HR research in the area of outsourcing has been focused mainly upon the impact upon the employees affected (Kessler *et al*, 1999; Rubery *et al*, 2004), especially those working in call centres. However, the reasons why organisations consider HR outsourcing remain under-researched, often generating contradictory evidence of whether cost or quality are the primary determinants. A number of unanswered questions remain in relation to how the decision to outsource HR is made and by whom; which HR activities are most likely to be outsourced; the nature of the contracts awarded to external providers, and the perceived underlying

reasons and consequences of this. These are some of the questions that have informed the research on which this Briefing is based.

> '*...drivers of HR outsourcing...[may include]...a desire to reduce costs, increase effectiveness, obtain external expertise or release internal HR expertise to focus on strategic issues...*'

## HR outsourcing in context

While outsourcing of HR activities is the focus of this Briefing, it is in fact only one response to a range of potential HR opportunities and issues. Other options for organisations (not covered in any detail in this Briefing) that might be considered as an alternative to, or as running alongside, outsourcing include:

◘ **Shared service centres**: the creation of an internal 'hub' for the delivery of HR services, to maximise economies of scale, often in conjunction with other services, eg these often focus on delivery of advisory services for staff and managers, and high volume transactional work. To date, the rise in organisations setting up internal shared service centres, appears to have been greater than *via* outsourcing.

◘ **Offshoring**: related to outsourcing is 'offshoring', which can be done on an outsourced or insourced basis, whereby an overseas operation is set up to deliver services back into the organisation.

◻ **Managed suppliers**: co-ordinating existing suppliers with an in-house 'contracts manager' (or similar), or creating sets of preferred suppliers with closer and longer-term commercial relationships. Companies often appoint external managing agents to coordinate a group of preferred suppliers, particularly in the area of recruitment and training.

◻ **Implementing an IT system**: this could also form part of an outsourcing project, as outsource providers can implement new IT systems without the organisation needing to invest in the technology themselves.

◻ **Employee self-service**: some organisations have in place comprehensive HR information systems that enable employees to undertake a number of HR-related activities themselves *via* a portal, without the need for any external intervention, for example, individuals updating their own personal details when their circumstances alter.

◻ **Buying in consultancy services**: although an organisation may decide to use professional advisers to assist in the decision and implementation of outsourcing, consultants typically advise on HR issues or implementation of processes but do not deliver or manage those processes, once implemented.

The CIPD would emphasise that outsourcing *must* be considered in the broader context of a range of options for improving the efficiency and delivery of HR services. We are carrying out a range of projects across this entire range of options which will result in future, related publications.

**Case Study**

**Building your own shared service centre – Standard Chartered Bank***

Standard Chartered Bank employs 33,000 people in over 550 locations, serving 56 countries and territories across the Asia Pacific region, South Asia, the Middle East, Africa, the United Kingdom, and the Americas. It is one of the world's most international banks, with employees representing 80 nationalities. Standard Chartered has effectively set up its own HR Shared Service Centre (HR SSC), which it runs itself from Chennai in Southern India.

Three main drivers influenced this decision. First, there was a desire to improve the quality of the HR service. This was followed by a desire to review and improve the structure of the HR function enabling it to deliver higher value. The third driver was the belief that the new set-up could bring significant cost savings.

Prior to the decision to create an 'in-house' shared service centre, various ideas around re-engineering the HR function were being considered. At the time there was a range of disparate HR processes and structures across the businesses. There was too much duplication of effort and time spent on non-value-adding activities and too little on critical areas such as engagement, performance management and talent development.

Outsourcing was considered briefly – in part to ensure the re-engineering effort reviewed all options and evaluated the merits for each, and also to look at what outsourcing providers could offer in terms of potential cost reductions.

Standard Chartered concluded that there was a strong business and technical case that its own people could 'do it better themselves'. The project began in Autumn 2000 with a thorough review of what would be required. Today, all people data across 56 countries is managed in the shared service centre. More complex, as well as standardised HR processes, are delivered from Chennai. In addition, over 50 per cent of employees are paid out of the HR SSC, and the HR SSC administers 27 pensions schemes across 17 countries, all employee share options and share schemes. There is also a sophisticated service on offer relating to employees' international mobility. Standard Chartered employees and managers from all over the world are also supported by a contact centre, which resolves their enquiries about these areas of HR activity.

International mobility and share administration are examples of the organisation's activities that have deliberately been brought in-house. Standard Chartered's experience is that with the new shared service centre, it is now able to deliver these services better – and for less – itself. More importantly, it has allowed Standard Chartered's HR function to focus on growth areas and invest in value-added services.

The bank has not experienced difficulties attracting talented people to work in its shared service operation in Chennai. There are large numbers of graduates looking for work. Many of those who work for Standard

Chartered have a Master's degree in Human Resource Management. The focus now is on looking in more detail at appropriate talents and on honing their strengths and skills for the best service delivery.

The technology underpinning the new style of HR delivery is PeopleSoft, complemented by Saba, from a Learning Management System (LMS). This incorporates employee and manager self-service and a limited number of more specialist modules, which have been built from the standard database. Internally, this overarching system is known as 'peoplewise'. The emphasis is on using single, standardised, processes around the business, which can be delivered *via* web-enabled technology.

\* Information supplied by Tim Miller and Luis Rojas.

## The difference between supplier and outsource provider

There may be some ambiguity between the terms *supplier* and *outsource provider*. For example, organisations have turned to recruitment agencies for years for provision of temporary labour and, in many cases, have formed deep, long-term commercial relationships. Is this the same as 'outsourcing recruitment'?

Referring back to the definition of outsourcing in the previous section is helpful in this respect:

*Outsourcing: the delegation of one or more business processes to an external provider, who then owns, manages and administers the selected*

*processes, based on defined and measurable performance metrics* (Gartner, 1995).

The difference between suppliers and outsource providers can be categorised according to the levels of ownership and risk.

'*Larger HR outsourcing deals are often described as "transformational" or "HR business process outsourcing" (BPO), having a significant impact on the organisation and touching every area of HR delivery.*'

Outsourced arrangements are characterised by:

◘ Increased levels of ownership by the outsource provider (of things like people, processes, technology).

◘ Increased levels of risk taken by the provider (through having accountabilities for direct employees and, in some cases, compliance and business outcomes) – where the purchasing organisation pays a premium to the provider for accepting these risks.

◘ Length of relationship (large outsourced deals are often struck for at least five years – however, this is less likely to be true for smaller arrangements with, for example, payroll providers).

◘ Integration with the purchasing organisation (a line manager or employee in an organisation will often be unable to tell whether the person they are dealing with is part of the provider or their own organisation).

Larger HR outsourcing deals are often described as 'transformational' or 'HR business process outsourcing' (BPO), having a significant impact on the organisation and touching every area of HR delivery.

What is outsourcing? › Potential drivers › Potential pitfalls and alternatives › Decision-making regarding HR outsourcing › Selecting outsource providers › Managing transition › Minimising the risk and making outsourcing work

◘ **The most common drivers for considering HR outsourcing**

# 2 | Potential drivers

*No company is going to approach us without a significant expectation regarding cost reduction. Cost reduction is always going to be a driver in this business. But ultimately, the work is about value added on an ongoing basis, and this requires the provider to be an extension of the client.*

Jim Madden, CEO, Exult, outsourcing provider

*Cost [was] the main motivation…*

(for BP) [FT 1 June 2004]

There are a number of drivers for considering outsourcing in general, both financial and more philosophical. For example, the UK Government is clearly imposing outsourcing of many functions as a means of delivering cost savings (eg as a result of the Gershon review and its focus on 'best value'). Similarly, within the private sector there are conintuing pressures to deliver improved shareholder value. Such wider drivers are likely to have knock-on implications on any drivers for HR-specific outsourcing.

Detailed below are some of the more commonly-cited drivers regarding HR outsourcing. While these stated drivers may be linked with various organisational benefits, it is, of course, the case that there are also solutions other than outsourcing that an HR function could adopt (eg internal shared service centre) that might deliver similar benefits. These alternative options are considered more fully in Chapter 3.

## 1 Philosophical reasons

Organisations that have a history of outsourcing other non-core activities (for example, finance, IT) may simply decide that HR is next in line for outsourcing. Similarly, sometimes an organisation may decide to outsource all non-core (support) services in one go, bundling HR, IT, finance etc together. In these situations the HR function may have a very limited voice in the decision-making process.

## 2 Reducing cost

This is the reported basis of most outsourcing business cases, because cost and profit are the most easily understood and measurable potential benefits. Outsourcing arrangements can result in cost reductions because:

- The outsource provider can apply advanced and continually updated IT systems to process data.

◘ The provider should have developed streamlined, simple, proven processes.

◘ The provider can have the advantage of economies of scale due to providing HR services for a number of employers.

◘ The provider can apply rigorous service management practices and focus.

◘ Fixed costs (eg investment in updated IT, headcount) can be replaced with variable costs, reducing working capital tied up and improving commonly used reporting ratios (eg turnover:headcount).

### 3   Reducing risk

Organisations may decide to outsource in order to reduce risk. This has often not been referred to as outsourcing, although it does fulfil all of the criteria. A company may hand over all elements of a process that might result in legal or cost risks, for example, writing of employment contracts, paying staff, working out income tax and national insurance contributions. In all of these cases, the organisation is paying the supplier both for their expertise and for the perceived reduction in risk resulting from this expertise. Outsourcing to reduce risk is particularly common where the

> *'...the organisation is paying the supplier both for their expertise and for the perceived reduction in risk resulting from this expertise.'*

process or resulting risk is specialist in nature (eg employment law).

> SPV Management, the UK division of an American company, decided to outsource the entire UK HR function, avoiding the need to recruit or train people internally to understand and deal with UK employment law issues.

### 3   Increase effectiveness of HR delivery

Outsourcer providers generally claim to be able to carry out HR processes more effectively than can be done in-house. For example, reduced recruitment timescales due to process efficiencies, mean that new staff, adding value and growth to the organisation, can be brought on board faster. Similarly fewer payroll errors may arise. Organisations may also embark on outsourcing to develop their revenue, profit or shareholder value, as well as to reduce costs. They can do this by using their external outsource providers to provide the expertise to add value to the organisation.

> CMi plc is a company that has grown rapidly (doubling in size to 160 staff in about 12 months). As the company grew, the directors needed to decide whether to increase internal capability, or to outsource. 'We decided to outsource HR because we felt that we did not have the capabilities in-house to deliver the required level of service for the new larger business.'

## 4   Providing expertise not available internally

For example, outsourcing compensation and benefits advice, or outsourcing top level recruitment, but retaining more general recruitment internally.

## 5   Moving HR up the value chain

Outsourcing aspects of HR administration has the potential to free up HR people to focus on strategy and business partnering. This desired shift in focus is the underlying driver of many outsourcing discussions and arrangements. Outsourcing can then drive the focus of HR delivery in organisations away from administration and service to a model driven by the desire to focus more clearly on strategy, policy and decision-making.

For example, a recent CIPD survey, 'HR survey: where we are, where we're heading' (CIPD, 2003), found that 46 per cent of HR employees considered administration one of their most time-consuming tasks, and 70 per cent said the same of providing process or consultancy support for line managers. Conversely, although 64 per cent of respondents identified *business strategy* as an important contribution of their work, only 17 per cent spent significant amounts of time in this area.

The activities that might create competitive advantage include those which:

◘   Are unique to the organisation.

◘   Can be demonstrated to add value to shareholders.

◘   Are non-replaceable (a competitor cannot achieve the same effect by using different processes or resources).

◘   Are non-transferable (a competitor cannot easily copy, steal or buy your approach or resources).

> Essex County Council needed to free up HR staff from day-to-day administration to work at a more strategic level. The organisation decided to outsource all recruitment administration work so that the HR department could focus on resourcing strategy – which builds the capability of the organisation as a whole.

## 6   To gain commercial return from HR resources

A few major UK outsourcing deals have been commercial (or joint) ventures, where an organisation has outsourced HR process delivery – together with a large proportion of HR staff – to service their original needs, but also, through process efficiency, to provide similar services to other organisations, with the outsource provider and original client both benefiting commercially. Alternatively, some companies have built internal shared service centres that could provide services to external companies as independent profit centres. It should be recognised that this focus on commercial return is difficult to do without a starting point of a strongly performing internal HR function, and even then will require significant investments to transform HR services from an internal, to a market-facing, focus.

> Siemens operated an internal shared service centre for their transactional HR activities, and decided to extend these operations. Their subsidiary, Siemens Business Services (working in collaboration with PWC Human Resource Services and Alexander Mann Solutions), now offers HR services to third-party organisations on a commercial basis.

## 7 Improved metrics

HR functions are under increasing pressures to prepare meaningful people management metrics (see CIPD's recent publication, *Human Capital Reporting: An internal perspective* (2004), for further details) They might think that outsource providers are best placed to develop these detailed metrics of HR processes which allow improved reporting – as part of balanced score card or other reporting system, for example.

*'Growth to certain critical sizes often prompts the organisation's leadership to make "recruit versus buy-in" decisions...'*

## 8 Change in HR leadership/HR expertise

New HR or organisational leaders with positive experiences of outsourcing HR in a previous organisation may wish to repeat the programme in their new employment. The differing context and activities of their new organisation need to be considered carefully. A similar situation is the loss of a key member of the HR team. For example, an in-house payroll expert might be difficult to replace at short notice, forcing the organisation to consider other ways of resourcing the activity. In this case, outsourcing of the single activity may make greatest sense.

## 9 Organisational growth

The organisation may be growing rapidly (organically or through acquisitions), placing strains on the existing HR provision. This is especially true of smaller companies, which may never have had formal HR provision. Growth to certain critical sizes often prompts the organisation's leadership to make 'recruit *versus* buy-in' decisions, and decide to build HR capability by outsourcing rather than by recruiting HR generalists (small company) or specialists (larger company). Similar arguments apply to organisations that are reducing in size (with similar temporary requirements on HR resources), or otherwise changing in a significant way (like new locations), which mean that their current HR provision is inadequate or unsuitable.

**Case study**

**Acquisition as a catalyst for outsourcing – SPV Management Ltd \***

SPV Management is a UK-based entity that was purchased in April 2002 by Wilmington Trust, an American Bank Holding Company, as part of its first foray into international acquisitions. The two organisations are of very different scales – as of the end of 2004, Wilmington Trust had approximately 2,400 staff, and SPV Management had 16.

Martin McDermott is the Chief Executive of SVP Management. He said: 'After the acquisition, Wilmington determined that outsourcing of our HR provision would be the best course of action in light of the complex UK and European HR legislation'. Interestingly, Wilmington in the USA does not outsource its HR. The outsourcing relationship was negotiated, and is managed on an ongoing basis, by a manager based in the USA. Being such a small company, SPV Management did not have any existing HR provision, so Wilmington chose a supplier to help it scope the contract and trial a service.

The outsourcing supplier, in addition to the services originally contracted for, has suggested additional HR services which could add value to the company. As a result of outsourcing HR, SPV Management put in place a 'baseline' HR provision for the first year, including staff handbooks, policies and procedures, and a review of contracts. 'In the second year of the relationship,' said Martin, 'we used our outsourcing supplier for more complex HR work including compensation and benefits consulting, and employee relationship issues'. Because SPV is a small company with high-value staff, a significant benefit of the outsourced HR arrangement is that it removes any distractions due to HR, releasing expensive employee time to focus on the core business.

\* Information supplied by Martin McDermott

What is outsourcing? → Potential drivers → Potential pitfalls and alternatives → Decision-making regarding HR outsourcing → Selecting outsource providers → Managing transition → Minimising the risk and making outsourcing work

◘ **Potential pitfalls of the HR outsourcing route**

◘ **Other strategies available to HR departments to improve their effectiveness**

# 3 | Potential pitfalls and alternatives to outsourcing

*86 per cent of internal shared services projects meet cost savings goals, compared with 67 per cent of outsourcing projects.*

HR Magazine, July 2004, p80

Outsourcing currently has a high profile as a solution to many HR issues and opportunities – and can be a sensible and valuable strategic choice for organisations. However, the fundamental issues and opportunities that outsourcing seeks to deal with can be solved with other alternatives. Even when outsourcing is the most appropriate approach it will usually not solve organisational issues on its own, but should usually be implemented in conjunction with other initiatives.

Table 1 on page 16 lists some of the potential HR issues, gives examples of underlying causes and then indicates a range of potential options available to organisations.

This chapter then moves on to examine some of the potential costs and pitfalls associated with outsourcing, and then to look at some of the alternatives to HR outsourcing that may result in similar benefits.

## Potential pitfalls of the outsourcing route

*Don't outsource what you don't understand.*

Randal Tajer, UBS Private Banking

Outsourcing is not a panacea. While the many potential benefits of HR outsourcing are evident and have been flagged in the previous section, it is important to recognise that, by itself, outsourcing will not necessarily solve organisational issues, and organisations should recognise that, if not carefully thought through, there might be some potential pitfalls. For example:

- Outsourcing can be 'like picking up spaghetti'. If your internal processes are poorly understood or overly complicated, then just transferring the same processes to the outsource provider is unlikely to provide any benefit. In this situation, either improve the processes before outsourcing, or accept that the provider will need to replace your existing processes wholesale with their own 'best practice' approach and that you will be less able to include your own particular nuances.

**Table 1** | Potential HR issues

| Human Resource issue | Possible underlying causes | Potential options |
|---|---|---|
| Need to cut costs of HR administration | No leverage of IT solutions, no common data sources. Inefficient, unnecessary or non-standardised processes. Poor economies of scale. Processes completed at unnecessarily high-quality levels. Expensive resources being used for basic processes. High ratio of fixed to variable costs. | Process rationalisation (stop doing things, or reduce quality). Internal process re-design. Shared service centre, with or without outsourcing. Offshoring. Web-enabled HR system. Outsourcing. |
| Need to access specialist HR knowledge | Existing knowledge is out-of-date. Knowledge is too expensive to hire on a permanent basis. Knowledge exists in the organisation, but is hard to access. Risks occur if a specialist is away or leaves the organisation. | Use of consultancy services. Create internal centres of HR excellence. Interim management. Knowledge-management solutions. Outsourcing. |
| Need to move HR accountabilities to line management | Cultural change to line managers having more responsibility for staff. Lack of HR resources to manage the employee relationship. | Job re-design. Change reward or performance structures for managers. Internal advice lines for managers. Outsourcing. |
| Need to make HR more strategic | Lack of clarity about what HR does. No board representation for HR. HT activities not reflecting organisation's needs. Administration tasks swamping HR, leaving no time for strategy formulation. | Revised delivery strategy for HR to enable the function to focus on strategic issues. Board representation for HR. Recruitment of strategic expertise. Greater investment in HR. Outsourcing might support the above options. |

◘ The cost savings from outsourcing are often largely due to the ability of the provider to leverage sophisticated technology through changing business processes to make them more efficient. If you already have good internal IT systems for employee data, the cost savings you can achieve by outsourcing may be reduced.

◘ Outsourcing does not absolve the organisation from good employee-management practices. The most important people management relationship – the one between a line manager and their staff – is retained in-house. While your outsource provider may be able to implement policies, advice and training to which you previously had no access, you will still need to work on manager–staff relationships.

◘ Outsourcing does not absolve HR leadership from the responsibility for delivery of HR practices and performance in the company. Although, in theory, Board Directors could speak directly to the provider about issues with HR process, people management, morale etc, in practice the HR leadership is still held responsible. In some cases it may be more uncomfortable to be held responsible for someone else's poor performance than for one's own internal department.

◘ Outsourcing does not automatically mean that line managers will stop using local HR people as the first line of support for queries and emergencies. In any major outsourcing arrangement, line managers will need to understand, accept and be trained to use the outsourced services.

> **'Outsourcing does not absolve HR leadership from the responsibility for delivery of HR practices...'**

◘ Outsourcing deals are often long-term and are normally based on assumptions about headcount, growth and organisational success. If, for example, economic factors force severe headcount reductions, then the deal may become loss-making for the provider and relatively costly for the outsourcing organisation. Outsourcing deals should take account of a wide range of possible future scenarios. A key challenge for both partners in an outsourcing deal is to find a way for the provider to replicate or improve the client's existing HR delivery, at a lower cost, while still being profitable.

◘ There is a risk of loss of local knowledge and ownership of HR processes. Sole ownership is likely to be more important for bespoke organisations.

◘ Potential risks might arise if the outsource provider offers a 'generic' solution with lack of tailoring to suit a particular organisation's needs.

**Case study**

**Deciding not to outsource – BG Group plc***

BG Group is one of the world's largest oil and gas companies, employing a core of 52,000 employees, with many more staff in joint ventures around the world. The company has used third-party providers for pension administration and payroll for many years, but has specifically decided not to consider outsourcing of any other HR functions.

All of BG Group's strategy and HR design is done in-house. It does use external partners for elements of recruitment and employee development, but retains all of the decision-making internally. Its rationale for this is that it feels its business is changing so quickly in terms of growth, markets and geographies that no outsourcing provider could keep up. Kevin Bishop is the head of Talent Management for BG Group: 'We don't feel that even the biggest outsource providers could do what we do any better. Rather than follow our competitors, we're actually less likely to consider an option that others are taking.'

BG Group actively pursues other strategies to improve their HR service delivery. 'We are using an HR intranet and central HR information system, but we need to explore how to make this flexible before we can extend its use', said Kevin. 'We have a very diverse set of people, in a very diverse range of roles, and it's this flexibility that gives us a competitive edge. We need our HR to be similarly flexible.'

BG's internal HR function numbers around 75 staff worldwide, of whom about 20 are involved in administration tasks and 55 in strategy, policy, decision-making and design.

* Information supplied by Kevin Bishop

To help individual organisations decide whether HR outsourcing might be an appropriate response to consider, they need to be aware of these potential pitfalls as well as all of the potential advantages that an HR outsourcing arrangement might offer.

They also need to be aware of the alternatives to outsourcing. The next section focuses on some of those alternatives.

## Alternative options

As suggested in Table 1, there are a number of alternative options that an organisation might consider if it wants to change the way HR delivers its services. Broadly, these strategies include:

◘ *Internal solution*. The HR function decides that it does not need any external assistance in achieving the desired changes in the HR provision. Possibilities include developing HR skills in-house, recruiting different HR skills, or building an internal shared service centre.

◘ *Internal solution with external support*. HR recognises that it needs some external support (eg consultancy services) to achieve the desired change. For example, if a decision is made to introduce shared service centre, external IT/ project management support might be used. Similarly, HR might request external support to develop a revised strategy that it will then develop and deliver internally.

◘ *Internal solution with limited external provision.* HR might consider that there are some aspects of its service that it wishes an external provider to deliver on its behalf. The possible reasons for this are covered extensively in Chapter 2, but examples might include, payroll and administration, pensions, or senior resourcing.

◘ *More extensive use of external provision.* HR might consider that it wants to make more extensive use of an external provider to deliver aspects of its service, eg using an external outsource provider to deliver all of its HR administrative activities. Again, the possible drivers for this are addressed in Chapter 2.

Ideally, all options need to be considered before any decisions are made to ensure that outsourcing is the most effective option for the organisation.

These alternatives also provide a baseline with which the benefits of outsourcing can be compared. Any analysis should include:

◘ The anticipated cost of current delivery.

◘ Different ways of measuring effectiveness of current delivery.

◘ Potential costs of moving from previous HR delivery to a new, improved level of delivery.

◘ Costs of ongoing implementation of the alternative delivery option.

◘ Financial benefit to HR of the alternative delivery method year-on-year.

◘ Benefit(s) to the business as a whole of the alternative delivery method.

Supplementary information on analysing different HR delivery options is included in Appendix 2.

Chapter 4 considers the whole decision-making process regarding HR outsourcing in more detail.

◩ **Reviewing existing HR provisions**

◩ **Considering what may be suitable for outsourcing**

◩ **Making the outsourcing decision**

# 4 I Decision-making regarding HR outsourcing

Having considered possible drivers, the potential pitfalls and alternative options, this chapter considers decision-making with respect to HR outsourcing. Figure 1, below, illustrates some of the questions that HR functions need to ask.

**Figure 1** I Do we need to change the way HR operates?

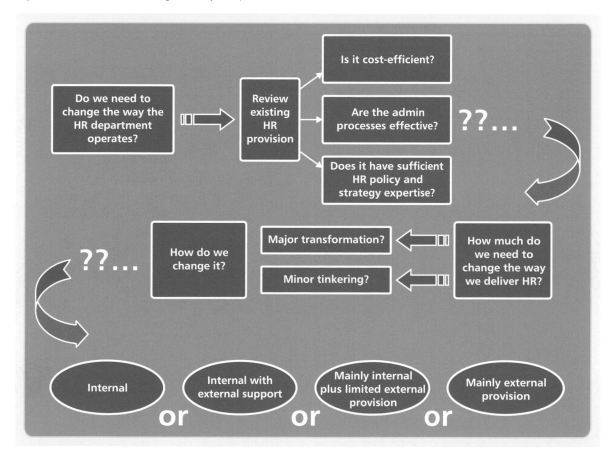

Decisions regarding whether to outsource HR activities must be taken in the context of the HR department's existing and desired contribution to the organisation's performance.

## Do we need to change the way the HR department operates?

Key questions to consider from the outset are:

a) what objectives does HR have to maximise its contribution to business performance?

b) In order to achieve these objectives, do we need to change the way the HR department operates?

> *'Most elements of HR activity have the potential for improvements, whether internally or via an outsourcing solution...'*

### Reviewing existing HR provision

In order to ascertain whether changing the way HR is delivered in the organisation could bring business benefits, it is necessary to review your existing HR provisions. Most elements of HR activity have the potential for improvements, whether internally or *via* an outsourcing solution – from strategic activities like organisational design, through to operational activities such as employee assistance programmes and payroll administration.

The following suggested questions can be used in relation to reviewing the organisation's various existing HR activities.

- How much does this activity cost us now? (overall, per employee, per transaction)

- How well is the activity working now? (Is the process effective?)

- Do we have sufficiently detailed policy and strategy in this area?

  (See the first stage of Figure 1.)

More detailed questions to help in this analysis include:

- What level of service do we actually need (ie speed, quality)? How does that relate to current performance?

- How highly do our employees value the activity?

- What is the risk of getting the process wrong? How much are we prepared to pay to avoid the risk?

- How unique are our processes? Could the activity be easily moved to a best practice standard without affecting the value added to the organisation?

◘ Does this activity currently add to the value of our organisation, or reduce it? (And how do we know?)

◘ Do we need to do this activity in a way that is specific to us because of our operating model?

◘ Does this activity need to be specialised in order to fit with our culture and values?

◘ If our competitors knew how we did this, would it matter?

◘ Does this activity contribute to building the core competence of our organisation?

As the questions above indicate, the degree of standardisation associated with outsourcing of HR activity will be an issue that organisations will be considering. Larger organisations – that are more likely to have multiple locations and divergent processes in different parts of the company – may see this as a source of concern. It should be noted that standardisation is an important respect in which providers of HR outsourcing suppliers are able to create economies of scale, and help your organisation deliver cost savings. The loss of some local control, therefore, is likely to be necessary, although this may not be palatable to all organisations. However, as suggested above, uniqueness is not always valuable. For example, having over 20 different payroll systems running separately across the organisation is unlikely be a source of competitive advantage.

### How much do we need to change the way we deliver HR?

Figure 1 demonstrates that a number of conclusions may be drawn from the review of existing HR provisions. A major transformation may be necessary, or perhaps only minor tinkering with existing HR provisions may be more appropriate.

> **'A major transformation may be necessary, or perhaps only minor tinkering with existing HR provisions may be more appropriate.'**

Conslusions could well vary across different parts of the HR function. For example, where the basic payroll may be functioning effectively, managing the employee share scheme or flexible benefits scheme could be more problematic.

### Options for improvements

As seen in Figure 1, options for improving HR delivery include undertaking changes that might be:

◘ internal,

◘ internal with external support,

◘ mainly internal plus limited external provision, or

◘ mainly external provision.

Chapter 2 contains details of the options for internal improvements that can be explored. It is important that these are considered alongside the option of drawing mainly external assistance, in the form of outsourcing. The section below is designed to help identify areas which could potentially benefit from outsourcing.

## Considering what may be suitable for outsourcing

HR outsourcing does not always mean putting all aspects of the function's delivery outside of the organisation. Much more commonly, organisations decide to outsource one or more components of the HR function. Which elements are outsourced will depend heavily on the organisation's size, situation, strategy and current assessment of HR performance.

HR activities can be broken down into four major elements:

◘ Developing HR strategy – deciding on the future direction and vision for HR and linking HR delivery to organisational objectives. This is usually difficult to outsource, as the strategy development will be highly dependent on the organisation's context and situation

◘ Setting policy and providing advice – giving guidance to managers and staff about how to access and use HR activities. Some policies, the ones which give guidance on how managers

need to comply with HR activities for legal or financial reasons, are usually common to a range of companies or industry sectors and may be standardised and outsourced. Other policy developments are a result of strategy and direction, and are likely to be more specific to a particular company's culture (and harder to outsource).

◘ HR transactional activity (eg screening candidates' application forms, processing employee change of personal details forms, administering the annual pay review). This area is usually most responsive to improvements due to standardisation, simplification and economies of scale, and is therefore typically the focus of outsourcing programmes.

◘ The management of the data used by HR activities – effective HR activity management depends on efficient data collection, manipulation, reporting and analysis. Data management is often outsourced without having that label; for example, few companies commission their own salary benchmarks. It is difficult to outsource a process without also outsourcing the related data, and outsource providers will usually have sophisticated IT tools to maximise the efficiency and value of data management. Most importantly, the provider will often have developed sophisticated tools for analysing and reporting on the data and will be able to supply advanced HR reporting for HR and line management.

Our research suggests that the more strategic elements of HR provision are much less likely to be outsourced by larger organisations. They are more likely to favour the outsourcing of transactional activities and the management of data. However the opposite is true of small organisations – strategy is just as likely to be outsourced as delivery, because there is usually little HR strategy capability in-house.

Figure 2, below, illustrates the range of HR activity associated with recruitment, and how these might be considered in terms of their suitability for outsourcing.

In the context of recruitment, an organisation may also define the boundaries of suitability for

outsourcing depending on the nature of the vacancy. An organisation may be willing to outsource more recruitment activity in relation to junior staff (for example, to include a provider carrying out telephone interviews or running assessment centres for front-line, customer service employees) but wish to maintain closer control and ownership over the appointment of senior managers.

Conversely, an organisation may wish to seek the assistance of a specialist external provider (such as a search consultancy) for senior positions, while filling more routine vacancies using internal resources, such as line managers, in conjunction with the HR team. The expertise of the organisation in the relevant area, the resources

**Figure 2** | Recruitment: an illustration of the range of HR activities that may be outsourced

available and the uniqueness of their approach will help drive decisions of this kind.

> *'Outsourcing decisions...are often based on assumptions about...future growth...(in terms of revenue, workload and, more relevantly, headcount).'*

## Making the outsourcing decision

### Clarify assumptions made

Outsourcing decisions and deals are often based on assumptions about the future growth of the organisation (in terms of revenue, workload and, more relevantly, headcount). These can be inaccurate. For example, a lower than anticipated headcount can make a particular outsourcing arrangement unprofitable for the provider and produce lower cost savings for the organisation. Making assumptions is usually a critical part of forward-looking business planning, but these assumptions should be clearly defined so that any decisions can be reviewed if situations change. For example, pricing models should be tested against high and low headcount estimates to test the sensitivities of predicted savings.

### Make a decision

This is about deciding which path (from the range of outsourcing routes and internal improvement options) makes most sense for the organisation.

It is important that both financial and non-financial considerations are taken into account when making the decision whether or not to outsource the proposed HR activity. Cost is likely to be a criteria, but you may decide to place high importance on flexibility of provision, for example, or alignment with drivers of core competencies. The connection with the organisation's strategy is crucial. Sometimes a cost–benefit analysis will produce positive figures, but HR outsourcing is entirely at odds with the organisation's strategy, ethos or culture. For this reason, cost–benefit analyses should be used to check the suitability of a decision, rather than to drive that decision.

## What might an outsourced model look like?

Two indicative examples of what the final model of HR service delivery might look like following a decision to outsource are provided below.

### A model of HR service delivery – large-scale

Typically, larger HR outsourcing programmes are focused on contact centre and back office processing centre activities. Outsourcing these elements will have an effect, not only on the internal HR processes, but also on the customers of HR (from organisational leaders through to potential employees) and the way in which expert HR knowledge is held in the organisation (eg through the forming and/or enhancement of centres of HR excellence). Therefore, it is important not to consider an HR activity in isolation, but

**Figure 3** | Illustrative example of a large-scale HR delivery model using an HR outsource provider

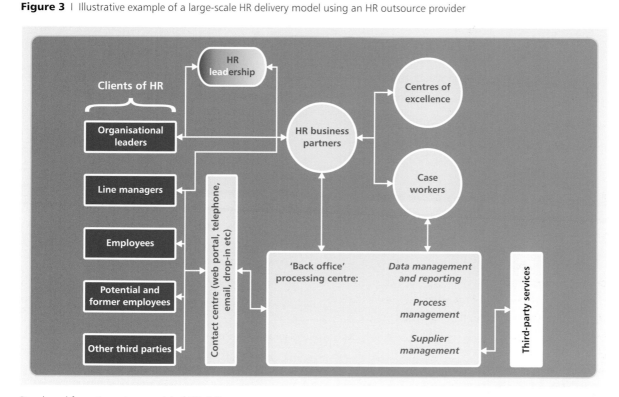

*Developed from Accenture model of HR delivery*

rather to think through how that activity will interface and affect other parts of the organisation. Figure 3, above, describes one possible model of large-scale HR delivery using an outsource provider (as shown in the lighter-coloured boxes).

**Case study**

**Deciding what to outsource – Essex County Council\***

Essex County Council decided to investigate outsourcing of HR in 1999. The Council needed to review and improve effectiveness and efficiency of HR provision, as a direct result of government insistence on providing best value to the taxpayer. Lorraine Pitt is the HR director of Essex CC.

In deciding what to outsource, Lorraine focused on transactional processes. 'We wanted to free up HR staff to work at a more strategic level, providing added value to the organisation', said Lorraine. The council already had external suppliers to deliver about a third of all recruitment processes, and over 50 per cent of training and development work. A proportion of organisational development work was also subcontracted to external consultants. In this environment, moving to an outsourced relationship for HR was easier because the organisation already had experience of managing HR supplier relationships – albeit on shorter timescales with less partnership.

Essex County Council decided to take the areas of HR that already had some element of supplier involvement, and move to a more complete outsourced arrangement. Now, the Council outsources all recruitment administration and a proportion of its recruitment selection work, and engages consultants in partnership to deliver its training strategy. It is currently considering the outsourcing of other areas.

When deciding how much of an activity to outsource, Lorraine needed to take into account the challenges of local government structure, which is two-tier with separate county and district councils. The outsource suppliers are starting to work with a range of stakeholders, and help the organisations to consolidate and co-ordinate HR services across the various parts of the county. Lorraine sees some risks in outsourcing: 'You need to be careful that the delivery of HR services by your outsource supplier does not get disconnected from your internal HR strategy and direction'.

When thinking about the future, Lorraine plans to develop HR provision in an interesting direction: 'Ideally, we'll move towards a model where the County Council offers HR services centrally to district councils, minimising duplication and reducing costs for the local government organisations overall.'

\* Information supplied by Lorraine Pitt

## A model of HR service delivery – smaller-scale

Of course, many organisations will only need to consider HR activities on a much smaller scale. In these cases a model showing the use of outsource providers might resemble the example shown in Figure 4, opposite. Smaller organisations may not have a specific internal manager with HR responsibilities, meaning that more attention would need to be paid to the internal relationships and accountabilities for the various elements of HR.

**Figure 4** | Example of a smaller-scale model of HR delivery using an outsource provider

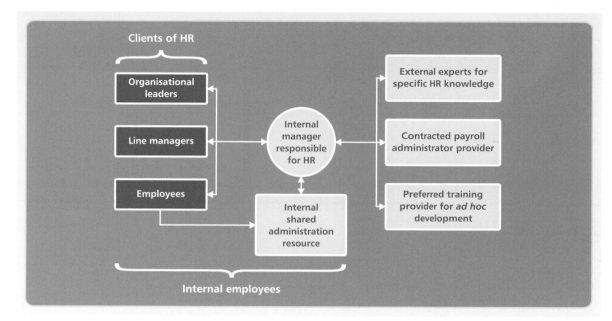

What is outsourcing? → Potential drivers → Potential pitfalls and alternatives → Decision-making regarding HR outsourcing → Selecting outsource providers → Managing transition → Minimising the risk and making outsourcing work

◘ **A standard process for selecting providers for an outsourcing project**

◘ **A checklist for deciding whether to use a single large provider or a range of specialist ones**

◘ **Guidelines on negotiating a deal**

# 5 | Selecting outsource providers

The process for selecting an outsourcing supplier is similar to the process for deciding on any other major partnership for the organisation. The sophistication of the approach and the level of decision-making needed in the organisation will, of course, depend on the size and scope of the programme. This chapter focuses on what makes outsourcing different to other provider selection activities. As previously mentioned, in many companies this activity may formally be carried out by a Purchasing or Procurement function. But, from discussions with the case-study organisations, it seems that the success of outsourcing relationships depends largely on good working relationships at all levels. It is important that the HR function, as the future manager of the relationship, takes a leading role (possibly working very closely with both IT and line management).

## A process for selecting providers

The process of identifying scope, providing a request for proposal and evaluating tenders is similar to that of other large-scale procurements. The main steps for selecting providers of HR outsourcing are set out in Figure 5 on page 32.

Some specific activities which could increase the likelihood of finding a good HR outsourcing partner include:

- Include, as part of the selection process, activities for evaluating other options (eg shared services, investment in existing HR capability) to ensure that outsourcing is indeed the best option.

- Identify a shortlist of potential suppliers – by networking with colleagues, desk research, attending exhibitions and asking specialists – before inviting a small number to produce proposals, to avoid being overwhelmed by inappropriate responses.

- Before selecting a supplier, visit other organisations that have already outsourced, in order to understand more about how the supplier works. Gather information from decision-makers and end-users about how the relationship is working, and what the benefits and challenges have been.

- Gather data about your existing HR provision, which you can use as a baseline against which

**Figure 5** | Selecting suppliers: a decision tree

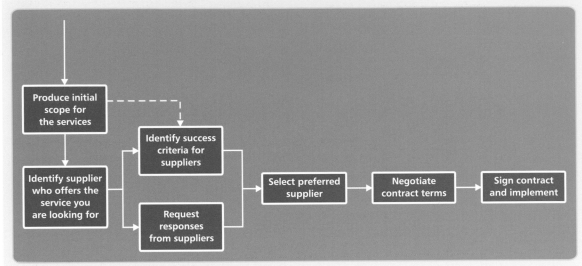

to evaluate other providers. This may also highlight any existing under-utilised HR capabilities.

◘ Include 'cultural fit' as part of your decision-making criteria. The HR outsource provider will need to understand, and be sensitive towards, your organisation's culture and situation.

◘ Consider desired length of contract. Because outsourcing relationships (particularly in larger deals) are often long term eg 5–10 years, it is crucial to be sure that the provider will remain in business for the proposed period.

**Case study**

**Selecting a supplier for HR outsourcing – Atos Origin***

Atos Origin, a leading IT services company provides consulting, systems integration and managed operation services to organisations across different industry sectors. It historically outsourced all of its temporary and permanent recruitment to a single supplier. After reviewing its previous recruitment service, Atos Origin decided to bring all permanent recruitment back in-house.

With the intention of obtaining an improved service from a specialist recruitment-outsourcing supplier, Atos Origin recently decided to re-outsource its non-permanent recruitment processes.

Interestingly, Atos Origin itself is an outsource service provider (of things like IT services, print and data services and payroll), so it did not consider outsourcing any aspects of HR in which it considered its own people to be expert and which it provides to third parties.

Their rationale for re-outsourcing non-permanent recruitment was as follows: typical of many companies, cost reduction was at the fore. However, it also wanted an improvement in service and process, resulting in better-quality candidates on board in a quicker time frame. It also looked for a supplier who could bring added scale, flexibility and further support to Atos Origin's corporate strategy, while reducing its fixed-cost base. In addition, Atos Origin needed to mitigate the legislative risks inherent in the engagement of non-permanent workers, and found that it could rely on the service provider's expertise on temporary worker contract

law and IR35 (laws on the employment of IT contractors). Matt Carr, as HR Strategic Buyer in Atos Origin's General Services Procurement team, worked as part of a core team comprising representatives from the Resourcing and Legal departments to select the supplier and negotiate the contract. 'We involved a range of internal stakeholders in the selection process, including the Senior Vice-President of HR, the Senior Vice-President of Finance, members of the Finance, HR and Resourcing departments, the heads of each business unit and other representatives who would be affected. Our Chief Operating Officer was the final signatory of the deal.'

The procurement team drew up a shortlist of nine potential providers by meeting with other companies who were clients of outsourcers, to get their view on what works and which providers would suit its business needs. 'It's incredibly difficult to find any literature on recruitment process outsourcing to help the research process', said Matt. 'We relied on talking to people and asking providers to present.'

All nine shortlisted providers were invited to tender, and the selection of providers from this shortlist was rigorous. A set of required competencies was drawn up and weighted, and the core team then marked each potential provider against these criteria to create a final list of four outsourcers.

Matt: 'Some of the criteria we used included innovation, the quality of the team, the professional accreditations held by individuals in the company (such as CIPD and SHL), customer references, financial track record, and marketplace credibility – we measured this by asking other companies for their reactions about the supplier.

We also tested each potential provider on their factual knowledge of HR, recruitment, resourcing and legal issues, and the way the account management would be structured. Cost was, of course, also a big driver.'

Atos Origin finally decided on Alexander Mann Solutions (AMS) as its non-permanent recruitment outsourcing provider. The negotiations included agreeing detailed service level agreements, covering a range of quantitative and qualitative measures right across the recruitment process, set to ensure the efficient delivery of a pre-screened and assessed non-permanent workforce to tight timescales. Their relationship is structured for five years, with an emphasis on continuous improvement, best value and market leading processes.

\* Information provided by Matt Carr

## Individual specialist, or 'one-stop shop'?

For larger outsourcing projects, the organisation will need to make a choice between selecting a full-service provider for all aspects of the outsourced HR delivery, or choosing a range of specialist providers and managing each one in partnership. This decision will always depend on a range of organisational factors including the level of service required and the resources and expertise in-house to manage relationships.

One further option is to consider a master vendor arrangement. This allows for a single organisation to manage a range of outsourced suppliers on behalf of its client, providing a single point of contact and taking advantage of the expertise of each 'best-of-breed' provider.

In practice, many of the 'full-service' providers will now also take on components of HR processing, and can be compared with the more specialist component providers, which blurs the distinction of the separate approaches somewhat. In theory, the advantages of each of the three approaches are shown in Table 2 opposite.

## Negotiating the deal

Organisations who have agreed successful arrangements with outsourcer providers tell us that time spent discussing and agreeing the scope and finances of the deal saves significant effort and complexities later in the outsourcing relationship. In particular, they recommend:

- ◘ Do involve procurement experts in your discussions. Outsourcing contracts are often complex business arrangements which will need expert legal and financial input.

- ◘ Do be clear about the assumptions that you make about your own organisation when deciding what services to purchase. The outsource provider will often develop a quotation, and build an infrastructure, based on your assumptions about volume of HR delivery (size of headcount, rate of turnover etc). If these assumptions are unclear or inaccurate, both parties may lose out. The contract should specify what happens if

**Table 2** | Relative advantages of different types of outsource provider

| A range of individual specialist providers | Middle option – master vendor arrangement | A single 'one-stop shop' outsource provider |
|---|---|---|
| ▪ Deep expertise in chosen areas. Usually a longer history of provision, so more experience. | ▪ Provide a single point of contact. | ▪ Scope for negotiation, and investment by the provider, based on overall higher value of the contract and often a longer-term relationship. |
| ▪ It is easier to un-bundle and back out of the arrangement if the outsourcing organisation's situation changes. | ▪ Can take advantage of the expertise of each 'best-in-breed' provider. | ▪ Reduces internal overhead in performance monitoring and management – only one supplier to deal with. |
| ▪ Scope for negotiation, based on deep process efficiency and volumes of the specific activity. | ▪ The master vendor will require payment for this, so the organisation needs to decide whether this activity is more cost-effective when kept in-house. | ▪ An opportunity to transform HR service delivery. |
| ▪ There is currently a greater choice of suppliers (relatively few 'one-stop shop' providers exist). | | ▪ The provider should understand the entire organisation's context. |
| | | ▪ The provider has a view of the end-to-end HR delivery and can, therefore, suggest through-process improvements. |

headcount or other assumptions prove to be lower or higher in reality.

◘ Do be clear about the level of service you need, and what you are actually buying. Do you need a basic HR administration function, or do you expect provision of expertise, consultancy and knowledge-transfer as well? Be careful about expecting one and paying for the other.

◘ Do agree the metrics that would be used to evaluate successful performance and how the provider will be rewarded or penalised for exceptional or poor performance. What remedies can be imposed, including contract termination? In large organisations, procurement or legal departments can help with contract definition and the potential provider may well have standard contracts to form a basis for discussion.

◘ Following on from the above point, do build flexibility into the contract wherever possible. It is very difficult to predict what services you will need over the lifetime of the arrangement, so a contract which allows an organisation to scale up or down in terms of volume or service level is useful. Do be prepared to re-negotiate a deal if experience shows that the relationship is not working as expected.

◘ Do expect the outsource provider to make a profit! The relationship needs to be based on a win–win scenario for both parties. If this does not happen, it is possible that outsourcing will not be so successful. The long-term nature of outsourcing relationships is better served by being clear about how the provider will be profitable, survive and grow during the life of the relationship, and how cost savings will be re-invested in service improvements.

| What is outsourcing? | Potential drivers | Potential pitfalls and alternatives | Decision-making regarding HR outsourcing | Selecting outsource providers | Managing transition | Minimising the risk and making outsourcing work |

- ◘ **The change management implications of an outsourcing project**

- ◘ **Managing stakeholders in the project**

- ◘ **Lessons learned about implementing outsourcing**

# 6 | Managing the transition from in-house provision to outsourcing

In theory, after the business case has been agreed, successful outsource projects are managed through four distinct stages:

◘ decision-making,

◘ supplier selection,

◘ transition,

◘ contract management.

In practice, the transition from in-house HR provision to use of an outsource provider is a significant change for the organisation, and needs to be managed accordingly. Clearly, the larger and more complex the outsourcing arrangement, the greater the need for clear change management skills. Current CIPD research on re-organising (*CIPD 2002, 2003, 2004, 2005*) has identified a number of common criteria that increase the chance of successful re-organising. For example:

◘ top level support,

◘ appropriate change team,

◘ HR involvement,

◘ project management disciples,

of which all will be relevant for different types of re-organisation.

In addition, an outsourcing arrangement will often also include significant changes to HR processes, (in a few cases, including HR self-service systems and/or formalised HR call centre provision for staff and managers). To highlight the scale of the change, Table 3, on page 40, compares 'before' and 'after' HR provision for a large project.

Note that this table mainly relates to larger-scale outsourcing projects. Smaller projects will usually have less far-reaching transition issues and change management, while still an important consideration, may be on a smaller scale.

**The outsourcing stakeholders**

The change of HR provision does not just affect HR staff and their direct internal customers. It is helpful for organisations to consider the effect of

**Table 3** | Comparisons of HR service pre- and post-outsourcing

| In-house provision | Outsource arrangement | Implication for change management |
|---|---|---|
| HR policies and processes are unique to the organisation. 'How we do things' is part of the culture. | HR policies and processes are standardised, and might need to be adapted. | Awareness and training for all staff and management. Culture change of 'new ways of working'. |
| Management of HR data may be on paper, HR IT systems may only be available to HR staff. | Self-service web-based HR management systems. | IT training for staff, potentially new IT equipment. Communication to explain confidentiality, access. |
| Line managers receive support from an in-house HR manager or specialist. | Line managers may need to interact with a contact centre, or allocated case workers for advice. | Clarifying and explaining how relationships have changed. |
| Line managers are able to contract suppliers individually for activities like training, recruitment. | Cetralised vendor management means that contracting for HR services needs to be approved by a central point. | Training and rewarding managers for using standard procurement processes. |
| HR team is permanent, internal staff. | Outsourcer provides staff to deliver contract. In-house staff may be transferred to outsourcer, or may be made redundant. | TUPE or redundancy programmes. Early communication to ensure affected staff understand what will happen to them. |
| In-house HR team has diverse roles. | The remaining HR staff in-house will have new roles, likely focusing on strategy, business partnering and supplier management. | New role descriptions for HR staff. Development programmes. Dealing with protential motivational effects of being 'the ones left behind'. |

the project on a wide range of organisational stakeholders, and ask:

◘ Who will be affected, and how?

◘ Who is likely to be in favour?

◘ Who might need to be convinced of the benefits?

◘ Who is now accountable for the relationship with each stakeholder, and does that relationship need to change?

## What might HR employees be asking?

The outsourcing project is likely to have greatest impact on the HR staff themselves. The types and scales of concerns will depend, of course, on the size of the outsourcing project. HR staff may pose some of the following questions:

◘ Who will I be working for in the future? (In-house, outsourcing company or somewhere else?)

◘ Who will manage me? What skills, behaviours and performance will be valued?

◘ How will my career progression change? What development will I receive?

◘ Who else in my work team will be affected?

◘ If I move to the outsource provider, will I just work for my previous company or will I work for a range of other organisations too?

◘ Will I have to relocate?

> '*The outsourcing project is likely to have greatest impact on the HR staff themselves. The...concerns will depend, of course, on the size of the...project.*'

## What might line managers be asking?

Line managers are often affected by HR outsourcing in ways that are not immediately obvious. Again, depending on the size and complexity of the outsourcing project, the following issues might arise:

◘ Who do I go to for what types of HR advice?

◘ Will this mean extra work for me? If so, how can I get support?

◘ Who can help me in various situations: eg grievance or disciplinary meetings, third-party provider disputes, staff training and appraisals?

◘ Will I have to carry out more HR activities myself?

◘ Will I have to use HR systems directly, rather than relying on my local HR person?

### Lessons learned about transition

Some common lessons for managing the transition from in-house to outsourced HR delivery include:

- Involve all of the major internal stakeholders in scoping the project, and continue to communicate with them about progress.

- Define and communicate the benefits of outsourcing to each of the stakeholder groups.

- Manage internal expectations – employees may expect the outsourcing project instantly to solve or remove existing problems, when in fact it may take a number of months to be fully performing (during which time service levels may actually drop).

- It helps to work with a well-defined team of in-house and outsource experts, with clear scope and remit.

- The transition period cannot be perfectly predicted – it may take longer than expected, and the configuration of processes and accountabilities may need to be fine-tuned during the transition.

- Be clear about who holds the knowledge about 'the way work is done here' and involve them in designing the new processes – manage the risk of them leaving.

- Be clear about who has the accountability for solving problems during transition. Is it the outsource provider or the outsourcing organisation? The original HR management cannot simply delegate to their provider. HR staffing may need to increase during transition, even though internal HR staff may be transferred to the provider.

- Avoid solving transition problems by reintroducing internal staff and processes that simply duplicate the new outsourced processes.

- Leave sufficient HR and leadership expertise internally to manage the outsource project and provider, and develop HR strategy.

| What is outsourcing? | Potential drivers | Potential pitfalls and alternatives | Decision-making regarding HR outsourcing | Selecting outsource providers | Managing transition | Minimising the risk and making outsourcing work |

◘ **The common risks that are a part of outsourcing HR activities**

◘ **Dealing with these risks and maximising the chances of a successful project.**

# 7 | Minimising the risks and making outsourcing work

*Everything is sortable if the relationship with Accenture [the outsourcing provider] is good.*

Jenny Arwas, BT

**Case study**

**Managing the ongoing relationship and getting best value from a central supplier of HR services – NU Healthcare, a subsidiary of Norwich Union Life\***

Aviva plc has 44,000 staff worldwide and provides insurance services through companies including NU Life, Morley Investments, NU Investments and NU Healthcare. An independent subsidiary called NU Central Services provides payroll, administration, facilities management, recruitment, helpline and staff pensions to all UK Aviva companies.

John Moules leads the HR team at NU Healthcare, responsible for around 1,600 employees. NU Healthcare, like the other companies in the Aviva group, purchases services from NU Central Services for an annual cost. So, even though there is no third-party outsourcing provider involved, from NU Healthcare's point of view, its HR administration provision is run along similar lines to an outsourcing relationship.

John tells us interesting lessons about how to manage the relationship between suppliers and customers of HR services. 'It's really important for us to balance our internal HR support to our managers with the outsourced support provided by our central services.

'We can't always use the external team to deliver all HR services to our line (even though we might be paying them to do that), because sometimes the knowledge needed to solve an HR problem is only held locally and internally. Therefore, it's important that some responsibility for HR delivery continues to be held internally.

'One of the risks of the HR outsourcing model is that if it's not managed effectively, it can damage the credibility of the HR provision. Even though services may be delivered externally, final accountability remains internal and HR cannot "walk away" from the more complex issues. The interaction between our internal customers (line managers and employees), our outsource providers and our own HR staff is a delicate balance.'

John also highlighted one of the potential disadvantages of an 'insourced' service (ie services provided by another part of a group): 'We have to work hard to ensure that our voice is heard. As one of the smaller subsidiaries in the UK there is always a concern to ensure that our needs are seen to be as important as those of the more substantial business units.'

\* Information supplied by John Moules

**Table 4** | Responsibilities for risks related to HR outsourcing

| Type of risk | Who takes the risk? | Risk avoidance plan |
|---|---|---|
| Service level agreements are not defined in detail. | Both outsourcer and organisation. | |
| HR strategy gets de-linked from outsourced HR processes. | Mainly organisation. | |
| Remaining HR staff do not have the skills to work strategically. | Organisation. | |
| Future organisation growth is not as expected. | Both outsourcer and organisation. | |
| Organisation's line managers ignore outsourced processes. | Mainly organisation. | |
| Parallel structures creep back into organisation's processes. | Both outsourcer and organisation. | |
| Accountabilities are not defined. | Both outsourcer and organisation. | |
| Poor choice of provider, unsuitable for scope of type of project. | Organisation. | |
| Outsourcer goes out of business. | Both outsourcer and organisation. | |
| Expectations are raised too high – project cannot provide the instant benefits promised. | Both outsourcer and organisation. | |
| Outsourcing is expected to solve internal problems which are not about processes. | Mainly organisation. | |
| Outsourcing project is expected to deliver continuously greater benefits/savings. | Both outsourcer and organisation. | |
| Outsourcer's choice (or imposition) of IT platform is not linked to client IT strategy. | Mainly organisation. | |

In this Briefing, we have already discussed the fact that outsourcing projects are always unique to individual organisations and are often unpredictable in their implementation. However, it is still possible to maximise the chances of success by identifying and planning for potential risks to the project.

Table 4, opposite, shows the major risks that were identified by the organisations included in the research, together with an identification of which party is likely to be most affected by the risk. Many of these risks are shared between outsourcing organisation and outsource provider – and this will provide one motivation for partnership working to minimise or eliminate the risks. An organisation considering outsourcing HR activities should think about which of these risks (or others) might apply to them, and document a specific plan for minimising or avoiding the risks.

Risk avoidance plans are likely to be organisation-specific to a certain extent, which will influence the possible solutions in each case. By way of illustration, for the risk example: 'organisation's line managers ignore outsourced processes' given in Table 4, a particular avoidance plan might include the following solutions:

- Up-front and on-going communication to all line managers.
- Training to all line managers (repeated as needed).
- Establishment of helpline and other support during transition period.
- Clear communication of impact (eg cost, duplication of effort) of non-compliance.
- Metrics (if possible) of extent of non-compliance.

## Tips for successful management of outsourcing projects

As with any project there will be a number of generic critical success factors (CSFs), such as:

- Managing the outsourcing arrangement as a formal project.
- Being clear and communicating rationale and goals
- Getting buy-in from employees and stakeholders.

Our research has also identified a set of recurring themes concerning the successful management of outsourcing projects, post-transition, that are detailed below.

- For large-scale arrangements, a joint project board (with representatives of both organisations) can be an effective way of reviewing and updating the outsourcing agreement.

☑ Consider splitting the project management role into two – one person accountable for managing the finances and contractual elements of the project, and a separate person accountable for the day-to-day management of the contract. This means that the day-to-day management can focus on building strong relationships while maintaining a high level of objectivity.

**Case study**

**Minimising Risks of Outsourcing – Cable & Wireless***

When Cable & Wireless (C & W) decided to outsource significant parts of HR, it wanted to transform its HR provision and add long-term benefit to the business. A range of transactional services was outsourced, leaving HR business partners retained in the business, together with senior specialists.

Ian Muir was a member of the senior HR team at C & W which agreed the resulting outsourcing deal with Accenture: 'Cost was, of course, a consideration and we really wanted to standardise and reduce duplication after a series of acquisitions. However, our focus was on transformation and e-enabling the organisation. It was a very ambitious plan and we could probably have managed it better – it was a journey of learning. Cost pressures on our business were accelerating and big losses were looming. We needed to downsize our HR staff by more than half after five mergers in the UK. We had a vision of transformation: better people, giving a performance edge and having global process consistency.'

C&W also wanted to increase HR's profile. In such a big and complex deal fulfilling a big and complex vision, there were many things that could have gone wrong. Ian gives a number of learning points for successful HR outsourcing implementation:

☑ Create a benchmark and really understand what you have before you consider outsourcing anything. A broken process will get worse, not better, if you outsource it. Only outsource processes that are working well, otherwise improvements or reductions in service cannot be demonstrated.

☑ Build a contract which has joint objectives and flexibility so that if you need to re-negotiate certain aspects you can – and are not locked into something that cannot work. Recognise that you might need to re-negotiate some elements and bring some services back in-house a couple of years later, if your situation and volumes change significantly. The contract will need to be profitable for both parties, even in times of unforeseen change, such as reduced staffing levels. This means it is essential to have very capable service managers on both sides of the partnership to manage and run the relationship. 'It's very difficult to get a balanced commercial relationship when there are unprecedented changes in the economic landscape. However, as a client, you must be clear about what you want, or you might find yourself paying extra for something that you don't need or value. Invest in service management and make sure its cost is in your first business case.

☑ If you are transferring experienced or knowledgeable HR people from your business to the outsource supplier, you need some way of capturing their tacit knowledge inside your own organisation. Otherwise you end up being over-dependent on the outsourcer for knowledge about your own business.

- Be very aware of internal stakeholder management during the process; be very open and candid about what is happening. Get dissenters on board as early as possible and do not ignore their voices. Be very clear about the 'sales messages' both to HR staff and to line managers, explain what the benefits of the outsourcing deal will be to them, and how things will change during and after implementation. Explain that these implementations take time to roll out, and issues will need to be resolved, so service improvements will not happen overnight. It is a journey, you will make mistakes – so prepare and learn how to manage your way through them.

\* Information supplied by Ian Muir

- Develop clear service-level agreements, and measure only those things which tell you something about the performance or value of the contract. A blend of qualitative and customer perception measures can be equally as valuable as quantatative financial and performance measures. Report on all these measures regularly – but bear in mind that outsourcing projects can fail due to over-measurements when the organisations lose sight of what measurements they can interpret or affect.

- Be clear that the outsource provider fits, or can adapt to, the culture of your organisation. The typically long-term nature of outsourcing means that cultural fit is an important factor alongside commercial and performance elements.

- Be confident about your relationship with your outsourcing provider, and work to develop (or change) relationships with individuals, if necessary.

- Ensure that there is a single point of contact in both provider and organisation who has full accountability for the outsourcing service. This is important in order to retain control, develop the relationship and respond to changes in business strategy and demands.

- The commercial elements of the outsourcing deal should ideally allow for sharing of risk and reward between the outsource provider and the client – if the project works well, both parties should benefit.

- As the scale of an outsourcing deal becomes larger, the need for specific change management skills grows more critical, too.

- Continue to invest in the development of remaining HR staff – and consider joint development programmes with the provider's HR staff to ensure consistency of communication and interaction with the line-management customers.

- Regularly review the use of HR processes, to ensure that the project is delivering the proposed benefits and that line managers and staff are actually using the new processes (rather than just 'ticking boxes').

- Create strong communication and knowledge-sharing links between the HR strategy team (assuming it has been kept in-house) and the process owners at the provider, to ensure that the processes and policies that are developed and delivered actually support the HR and organisational strategies.

- Pay attention to the elements of HR provision that may still need to be improved inside the organisation, and which were not intended to be addressed by the outsourcing project.

- Be clear about when and how line managers and staff can contract for added-value consultancy services, and when the provision is only for basic administration tasks.

**Case study**

**BT: the next 10 years***

BT has recently announced that it has renewed its HR outsourcing contract with Accenture HR Services for a further 10 years.

As the initial five-year contract came up for renewal, BT considered a number of different options, but re-chose Accenture based on their sustained performance during the previous 24 months, the Accenture HR Services global delivery capability and the wider strategic relationship that exists between BT and Accenture. Most importantly, BT was confident that Accenture HR could continue to deliver against BT's requirements. At present, BT's internal HR function operates with some 500 employees, largely operating as strategic business partners, focusing on value creation for BT through innovation and transformational activities.

BT was itself looking to move its whole method of HR service delivery into new territory over the coming years. First, it is introducing Peoplesoft 8 in the next couple of months, which will be the first time that it has operated a self-service delivery model for HR services. BT believes that the close links between its own HRIS and the relationship with Accenture are pivotal. Second, it is looking to extend its HR outsourcing delivery to its non-UK operations, which will impact upon the 10,000 employees outside the UK. In order to provide a service to these overseas operations, BT will make use of Accenture's overseas service centres in Bangalore, Bratislava and Chicago as well as the UK centre.

As BT enters into this new deal it has put in place a number of performance criteria and metrics that reflect the outcome-based service it is looking for Accenture to deliver. In part, this reflects a recognition from both sides that these were not so well-defined during the early part of their original contract. They believe the key factor that will ensure the success of this new contract is the relationship BT has with Accenture.

* Information supplied by Jenny Arwas

# Appendix 1 | HR outsourcing glossary

The following is an explanation of some of the most common terms associated with HR outsourcing.

**Application Service Providers (ASPs)** – an ASP provides an HR software solution over the internet and 'rents' this to companies. These software solutions can often manage payroll, benefits, employee data and others, without the organisation needing to implement and manage the software in-house.

**Business partner** – an organisational role that acts as a link between the HR department and line managers, responsible for ensuring that HR activities are aligned to the needs of the organisation. These roles often report *via* the line-management structure with dotted-line relationships back to the HR department (or *vice versa*).

**Business Process Outsourcing (BPO)** – a phrase that applies to all outsourcing, not just HR. BPO is the transfer of responsibility for an entire process (eg the recruitment process) to an external company. The external company usually determines how the process operates, as long as the outcomes of the process conform to the organisation's requirements.

**Case work/case workers** – where HR functions operate a shared service centre model (see *Shared service centre*, below), it is common for queries to be of different types, ranging from simple queries that can be dealt with immediately by the initial point of contact, to those that relate to more complicated issues or 'cases', that will be referred to HR experts or 'case workers'. An example of a 'case' might be a query relating to a disciplinary procedure that might be dealt with *via* a 'case worker' who has expertise in legislation relating to employee relations.

**Component outsourcing** – outsourcing single, discrete elements of HR activity (for example, the *recruitment* component, the *training* component, the *payroll* component etc).

**Contact centre** – a function often offered by larger outsource providers, where all employee and manager queries about HR (whether by phone or email) come into a central point – the contact centre – for initial response or handing over to HR specialists.

**Human Resources Information System (HRIS)** – an IT system which holds data about employees and HR activities. May include 'self-service' to allow employees and managers to update data themselves rather than asking a central HR administrator to do this. Larger HR outsourcing programmes often include provision of leading-edge HRIS applications.

**Key Performance Indicator (KPI)** – KPIs are the individual measures of performance that the outsource provider agrees to measure, report on and work towards. For example, a KPI might be '100 per cent of staff paid on time and accurately', or '95 per cent of recruitment applications acknowledged within five days'.

**Master vendor agreements** – a large outsourcing programme may involve many individual supplier organisations. It is common for one of these suppliers to take the lead in managing the outsourcing contract – this supplier is then called the 'master vendor'.

**Offshoring** – an overseas operation set up to deliver services back to the organisation. Offshoring has been used for lower-value work

(processing of payroll, for example) in the past, but is now increasingly being investigated for higher-value work like CV screening, developing e-learning courses etc.

**Service Level Agreement (SLA)** – usually a part of the formal outsourcing contract, an SLA is a definition of what levels of service the outsource provider will work to, including cost, quality and timeliness measures.

**Shared service centre** – this term is sometimes used interchangeably with contact centre. It refers to a central administrative centre that has been set up as the initial point of contact for all employee HR-related queries.

**Self-service (employee self-service)**. Some organisations have in place comprehensive HR information systems that enable employees to undertake a number of HR-related activities themselves *via* a portal without the need for any external intervention.

# Appendix 2 | Analysing different HR delivery options: supplementary information

Chapter 3 of this Executive Briefing provides some high-level criteria that any analysis of different delivery options should include. In this Appendix we provide further examples to help organisations undertaking this analysis.

- The anticipated cost of current delivery – using figures for a number of previous years to give a true picture of baseline costs. Costs should also include accommodation; share of IT infrastructure; recruitment, training, development of HR staff, and the costs of all existing third-party suppliers. If cost data is unavailable then assumptions and estimates can be made provided the basis for their estimation is fully explained and justified.

- Measures of current delivery – the deal will undoubtedly include critical success factors and service level agreements (SLAs), which need to be based on a sound foundation of current measures of service delivery. The CIPD's publication, *Human Capital Reporting: An internal perspective* (CIPD 2004), provides useful additional information on the importance of, and ways to measure the contribution of, people to the business.

- The cost of moving from the previous HR delivery to a new, improved delivery – which may include: IT costs (software and hardware); the costs of developing and implementing new processes (including re-engineering processes, creating new policies and documentation if necessary); change-management and communication; training of staff (including line managers) to use new processes, and any potential severance payments.

- The cost of on-going implementation of the outsource programme – including the actual amounts payable to the outsource provider, as well as the cost of managing the provider. Charges may vary according to volumes of transactions, headcounts or performance, so low and high extremes should be modelled.

- The financial benefit to HR of the option year-on-year – how much money will the organisation save each year when the outsourcing programme is up-and-running? What does it plan to do to release this money and use it effectively? (There is a danger that, if there is no plan to surface the financial benefit with clear action plans, then it will be lost due to duplicate work and returning inefficiencies.)

◘ The benefit to the business as a whole of the option – for example, improved absence management, improved time and attendance capture.

◘ Other non-financial benefits of the option – for example, improvements in process quality.

# References and further reading

## References

**CHARTERED INSTITUTE OF PERSONNEL AND DEVELOPMENT (2003)**

*HR Survey: Where we are, where we're heading*. Survery Report. London: CIPD.

**CHARTERED INSTITUTE OF PERSONNEL AND DEVELOPMENT (2003)**

*Reorganising for Success: CEO and HR Managers' perceptions*. Survey Report. London: CIPD.

**CHARTERED INSTITUTE OF PERSONNEL AND DEVELOPMENT (2004)**

*HR and Reorganisation – Managing the challenge of change*. Change Agenda. London: CIPD.

**CHARTERED INSTITUTE OF PERSONNEL AND DEVELOPMENT (2004)**

*Human Capital Reporting: An internal perspecive*. London: CIPD.

**CHARTERED INSTITUTE OF PERSONNEL AND DEVELOPMENT (2004)**

*Reorganising for Success – A survey of HR's role in change*. Survey Report. London: CIPD.

**GARTNER REPORT (1995)**

'Outsourcing – 14 Critical Success Factors'. In *Business Issues*, Feb 1995.

**MOLLOY, E and WHITTINGTON, R (2005)**

*HR: Making Change Happen*. Executive Briefing. London: CIPD.

**KAKABADSE, A. and KAKABADSE, N. (2002)**

'Trends in outsourcing: contrasting USA and Europe'. *European Management Journal*, Vol. 20, (2), pp 5–19.

**KESSLER, I., COYLE-SHAPIRO, J. and PURCELL, J. (1999)**

'Outsourcing and the employee perspective'. *Human Resource Management Journal*, Vol. 9, pp 5–19.

**KLAAS, B.S., MCLENDON, J.A. and GAINEY, T.W. (2001)**

'Outsourcing HR: the impact of organizational characteristics'. *Human Resource Management*, Vol. 40, (1), pp 92–101.

**LAWLER, E.E., ULRICH, D., FITZ-ENZ, J., MADDEN, J. AND MARUCA, J. (2004)**

*Human Resources Business Process Outsourcing: transforming how HR gets its work done*. New Jersey: Jossey-Bass/Wiley.

**RUBERY, J., CARROLL, M., FANG LEE COOKE, GRUGULIS, I and EARNSHAW, J. (2004)**

'Human Resource Management and the Permeable Organization: The Case of the Multi-Client Call Centre'. *Journal of Management Studies*, Vol. 41, (7), pp. 1199–1222.

**WHITTINGTON, R and MAYER, M (2002)**

*Organising For Success in the twenty-first century: A starting point for change*. Research Report. London: CIPD.

## Further reading

There are many books available about outsourcing in general, and also specifically about HR outsourcing. These include:

**CORBETT, M.F. (2004)**

*The Outsourcing Revolution – Why it makes sense and how to do it right*. Chicago: Dearborn Publishing.

**LAWLER, E.E., ULRICH, D., FITZ-ENZ, J., MADDEN, J. and MARUCA, J. (2004)**

*Human Resources Business Process Outsourcing: transforming how HR gets its work done*. New Jersey: Jossey-Bass/Wiley.

**VANSON, S. (2001)**

*The Challenge of Outsourcing Human Resources*. Spiro Press